SOUL MUSIC

poems by

Laura Lee Perkins

Finishing Line Press
Georgetown, Kentucky

SOUL MUSIC

Publisher: Leah Huete de Maines
Editor: Christen Kincaid
Cover Art: Laura Lee Perkins
Author Photo: Laura Lee Perkins
Cover Design: Elizabeth Maines McCleavy

Order online: www.finishinglinepress.com
also available on amazon.com

Author inquiries and mail orders:
Finishing Line Press
P. O. Box 1626
Georgetown, Kentucky 40324
U. S. A.

Table of Contents

SOUL MUSIC is a word composition of poetry.
Echoing the emotions and sounds of life in Maine and Arizona through word paintings, **Soul Music** embraces operatic components.

I. PRELUDE

Ushered

Your language   in-my-face   tonight
Like jet-black hair   dipped in blood.
Your truth screamed   through charm and wit
Whispering codas into the microphone
as a lover
whispers
in the beloved's ear.
"Come, join with me."

Your wares' delivery package
beautifully wrapped
in compassion and sincerity.

Words lining my heart with velvet
Like jet-black hair   dipped in blood—
The red and black of the Scorpio's world.

Patient Leo Lion . . . . . . waiting to pounce
devouring indifference.

The ride into fame rolls in your aura
As you silence us into the Feast of Knowing
the Feast of Fulfillment.

In mesmerized anticipation
We were ushered across the barbed wire border,
Escorted into both sides of your open heart.

Inspired by Luis Alberto's reading at the University of Arizona in Tucson.

3

The Marriage Coffin

He left her—
Back into the marriage coffin
With two matching death-mate chairs
Seated in the *living* room of the dead.

Silence and guilt rule in this virgin white box
Housing his infidelity.
Only the blaring television hides the grief
Silenced by decades of loneliness and deceit.

His groping, hungry hands screamed truth,
Knifing reality into the silence
of her heart's night.
The cries reverberated, echoing
familial generations of disbelief,
betrayal and rejection.

His heart also wept
as his eyes bled love
deep   deep
into her soul's open wounds.

Love, when abandoned,
Wanders aimlessly through the years,
Calling forth with wretched longing
from the full moon's breast,

Boomeranging love's light   between them
for   eternity.

II. STAGING

Misty Pine Forest

The mist
seeping through the pine forest
envelopes us—two.
Tenderly
caressing our faces
as we turn to look into each other's eyes
Hiding us from all
but the rising within.
My female being warms and swells
in your presence.
Our hands join
in welcome anticipation
Calmed
with inner peace.

Soul Warming Sun

Soul warming sun
Streaming through magnificent oaks
Onto virginal paper.
Surrounded by penetrating warmth
I relax into knowing.

Calmness spreads—
Melting butter flows in my veins
Inner struggles cease, merging all.

Empty bench beside me—filled
with quiet, kindred spirits
Content with this scene.

March in Maine

For months upon months
My feet have not felt these shifting beach sands.
They've been busy gripping icy paths
As my ears longed for sounds of breaking surf.

Today our prison door is unlocked
A one-day pass into Spring.

I walk in damp, seaside winds
I rest on winter's beach remains—
battered trees and storm debris.

Listen—the snow is melting—dripping
Freeing the sand dunes for terns
To return—Sunday's free ticket to JOY.

Clapping my hands in appreciation
I step into Spring's new growth of creativity.

Summer

The gentle breeze in my hair,
Warm, ripe sun upon my face,
The scent of fresh grass smells so good!
There's so much summer to embrace.

Summer is truly abundance,
It is love in full bloom,
Bringing memories of former times,
Summer erases boredom and gloom.

Many of my personal treasures
Stored deep within my soul
Are really very simple events,
Held in my memory bowl.

Like a baby's first breath,
To hear her soft cry,
To touch her soft skin
As I hum soft lullabies.

To smell newly baked bread,
To feast on homemade jellies,
To pick the summer's first tomatoes
And a picnic to fill our bellies.

To open the windows, curtains bellowing,
To smell the clean, country air,
To lay on a beach blanket in the sand
Or jump in the lake—on a dare.

Summer can be lazy
And filled with fun in the sun,
Summer brings joyous reunions
Packed with friends, family and fun.

In the midst of all the memories
Of picnics on a full-moon, illuminated night,
The inner sense of gratitude exudes
Turning our souls back to the Light.

Back to Love and Spirit,
Our true, animating Force,
Infinite Intelligence moves through us
As our guide—our divine Source.

The Old Split-Rail Fence

The old split-rail fence
Is bent and very weathered,
Leaning toward the bare ground
Upon which it is tethered.

Like an old, aged person
It appears very worn
With no hope for recovery
Except to be reborn

Into a new existence
Maybe the fence into a table?
Like a person into spirit form
When their death transition is able

To carry the soul—lift it up,
Bringing a new world into view—
Someday we'll all be transformed
From the old into the new.

Late September Sun

Late September sun
Warming my soul,
Seeping into my bones.

How to contain a few ounces
Of your warmth
To savor
In frigid January
When bitter winds
Freeze the blood in my veins,
Chilling my creative spirit
Along with the tender flesh.

Autumn's Song

The breathtaking colors of autumn
Shout from the mountains nearby,
"Don't forget to gaze at us!"
As we humans heave a sigh.

The beauty is overwhelming
The painter must be well-pleased,
As we survey the finished work
Of Earth's dying grasses and leaves.

Their season's life now seems so short
But what a glorious way to go!
A burst of yellow, orange and red
Before all is covered with snow.

The pines remain green all year
To help us remember May
When new green sprouts start pushing out
In their slow, methodical way.

Fall slips by so quickly
Winter days often drag on
As we wait for spring's soft lullaby
So different from fall's full burst song.

Full Moon

Full moon—
Canon exploding the night sky
Rising over silent, dense pines.
Perched on the deck in anticipation
Sounds of summer nightfall
Fill my soul with memories
Called forth from forever.
Pulsating rhythms echo
Glory, laud and honor to Thee.

The deck altar candle warms my heart—
Held in your right hand
Beating   slowly   to the breath

      of my desire

To melt into the moon.

Heron

Gliding gracefully over the still pond
The heron keeps a watchful eye—
Tuned with a deep awareness
As a perceived enemy passes by.

Pausing under a protective tree
Heron stretches to a full state of alert.
Observing the enemy with guarded pause
Heron settles back, back into the dirt.

Watchful as possible enemies appear
The heron almost sighs as it stands
And gracefully floats away from the shore,
Away from the enemy   called man.

Soul Music

The first dusting of the winter ground—
Fresh tracks on the forest floor this morning.
The cleared path gleams white,
Shining above late fall's brown leaves.

Dense trees
Barren grey branches stripped naked
by the loss of daylight,
Standing, patiently waiting
for winter's white blanket.

Resting during freezing months of darkness
They wait for spring's renewal,
Holding abandoned nests of hope
The trees sway and groan.

A sentinel hawk looms overhead.
Prey is easy to spot in the November woods,
Frightened by the sounds of hunters' guns.
Peering through the window above my desk
My mind is allowed freedom to roam
Through forests of written language
Turning words into music of the soul.

Icy Memories

Snow   resting heavy on the branch of my
memory tree   cold   wet   heavy.

Longing for the sunshine of a new season,
Bending under the weight of the past,

I age forward into spring
with increasingly cautious steps.
Icy memories are slippery, cold, frozen
and could cause catastrophic falls
into a terrifying hell.

Fragments

Fragments of winter
Fragments of spring
Fragments of glorious
Indescribable things.

Snow-covered pond
Budding young trees
Birds trilling soft songs
A sun-drenched, warm breeze.

Tired winter muscles
Long to run up the hill
The mud-covered pine needles
Will slip you a thrill!

I sit on the bench
Eating lunch in the sun
Winter's retreat very welcome
Spring's persistence has won!

Written in late March at the Bates College Pond

III. RECITATIVE

Shame as My Raiment

Cloaked in shame
Passed down as a treasured family heirloom
A garment which the family recycled

    over and over and over.

Inherited by default.

Invisible fabric   woven by the Devil
from secrets, lies and deceptions.

Therapy, hypnosis, direct encounters
pulled apart defiant threads,
Tightly interlaced–taut from generations of
pretense and affectation.

Lonely, cold, solitary
with shame as my raiment,
cloaked in a garment offering no warmth.

Exposed. Naked.

Until all threads were unraveled,
separated and carefully examined,

Loom hovering before me—waiting
As I labored, learning the necessary skills
to weave a robe of dignity and self-respect.

Created by acceptance and forgiveness—
Satin-soft   velvet-warm

Woven from blood-red strands of Truth.

Living Behind the Lie

Living behind the lie
My identity—screened
from others and myself.

Darkness kept the secret safe.

Light … forbidden to enter
the depressive sanctuary.

"We must never tell!"
warned the jail-keeper.
Someone might get hurt.

(Someone already hurts!)

Who is that someone?
A woman no one knows,
Hidden behind the finely woven
fabric of deceits and lies.

She knows not herself

Ancient Graves

Whispers of silence
Voices beckon from centuries past.
Ancient spirits, your graves
Rest deep within my heart.

Your love surrounds me
Enfolding me in angels' wings

As I waltz with ghosts
To music that is no longer playing,

Reverberating within the silence of forever.

In the Valley of My Soul

In the valley of my soul
I wait to be inspired
I wait to hear Spirit's voice
At night when I am tired.

Until the first canyon rays
Of early morning's light,
I listen, remembering the magic
of my wandering dreams last night.

Deep within my humanness
A soft tender glow seems to shine,
I long to fan the spark's gentleness
To connect me back to Thine.

My heart beats so steadily
Within the fullness of my chest,
Rhythmical, summoning, it calls me
To bring forth my very best.

And then I feel the warmth of nature—
The knowing of a presence nearby,
I listen and hear rustling sounds …
Birds' wings—I start to cry.

I know the oneness of ALL on earth,
The inner-connectedness we share.
Human stewards of this land
Entrusted to demonstrate care.

As we dance lightly upon the Earth,
Looking down into the canyon's abyss
Trying to comprehend creation's power
While we ponder the unusual tryst

Between animals roaming the land
Birds and insects flying in the air,
Fish swimming in the waters below
Endangered species calling "Please care!"

You are entrusted with our future,
It is upon your shoulders, you see
The future of the planet Earth
Is your re-spon-si-bil-i-ty.

You carry the burden of liability
You're yoked with the burden of truth
To make sure clean air, water and land
Are understood by the precious youth.

Nature never withholds its beauty
Nature never stifles its song
But we, the stewards of the earth,
Have been silent far too long.

Each one of us needs clean water
And soil that is chemical-free.
Rachel Carson, writing from Maine,
Told us this—clear-ly.

The earth is precious and fragile,
Nature is our greatest teacher.
We must monitor Mother Earth's heartbeat
Listen to the language of her creatures.

She offers us everything we need,
But we have continued to rape
Her land, air, water and forests
Why do humans continue to desecrate

The Earth, which supports us so gently,
Asking for nothing in return
But to love, support and cherish us
Until we are finished—ashes in urn.

The Power of Acceptance

Your letter arrived today—
My soul was waiting,
Reduced and elevated to tears of joy
by your responses to my Word Songs.

You—the magnificent interpreter
of musical symmetry tripping over the ears,
Resounding silently in the heart.

Nice to imagine that my writings
offered scenes to expand your mind.

Nothing less than thrilling,
A miraculous awareness
of the power of acceptance.

Once I read a short poem to a friend.
The response silenced my soul for weeks.

"I don't get it," she replied into the pregnant
silence.
Like a severed umbilical cord my creative
juices
Withered . . . my soul wilted and dried—a
barren desert.

Today your words watered my thirsty soul
and I feel eternally grateful to you.

I Am Not

I am not a plant that can be torn

     from the ground,

Uprooted by your sweeping winds.

Why?

Why do I dream so many dreams?
Why does my mind run so free?
Is there no lid to clamp on my thoughts
To keep them inside of me?

When I strive to hide my feelings
They pour out every which way—
If only I had longer to process them
A waiting place for them to stay.

Why do I feel so much so deeply
When others seem to take life in stride?
There must be an alcove somewhere
For a few strong feelings to hide.

Life's Laundry

Soul communing with Nature,

Singing a beautiful melody

Propelled by a silent rhythm.

Pulsations driving, pushing,

Stabbing truth deep into consciousness—

Wringing written words from my heart,

Hanging life's laundry

      on the public clothes line

For all to see.

IV. ARIA

Flooding

The Muse has arrived!
Bone-dry desert riverbeds of consciousness
Finally cleansed   by the Monsoon Muse.

Dank scents wet my heart's parched floor
Filtering through my nostrils—
Like fresh-cut hay.

The Muse arrived in a downpour of awareness
Summoned by the clanking bones of my skeleton.

Strong bourbon on an empty stomach
She offered a drink from the elixir bottle of Hope.

Quivering   I experienceded labor
          and rebirth.

Supplication

I ask not to be honored with beautiful life experiences
But pray for the personal strength and fortitude to endure,
To not cave in under the explosive weight of rejection—
To not crumble into the ashes of flaming memories.

I want to live in the sunshine of Hope,
Satisfied with insights gained from living within the moment.

All my wanting cannot erase the past.
All my insistency and trying to understand
cannot project a pain free future.

How to learn from the past when I'm frozen, cold and immobile—
Frightened to share myself with others.

Do with me as You will, Great Spirit,
For your will is what I want to live.

Tears

Tears stream down the window of my face,

       Irrigating dried seeds of emotions

Smearing the mirror's memories

       Sounds breaking open the parched silence of my heart.

Each footstep inches me closer to my past,

       Coming full-circle into the deep freeze of my future.

Waiting for the warm touch of your eyes

       To melt the icy silence into knowing.

V. CABALETTA

Children's Voices

Sounds of children's voices rise
from the hard, artificial blacktop playground

Bubbles bouncing across the tar
They race.

Unbottled from the caged classrooms
they run, shout, fight, laugh.

A few secrets are whispered
As others stare into nothingness.
Recess is ecstasy for some
Loneliness for others.

The production line of education
Leaves so many wanting
Imagine their feet longing
For soft, grassy spaces to explore –

Children yearn for recess
while I yearn to learn.

Naked Writing

I write naked, unclothed
To expose the flesh of my heart
Ruminating under my skin
Through silent penned weeping and joy.

I write about friendships that pulsate
With the petulance of younger days.
How precious these revival meetings are!
Connections so deep with longing
Gushing with welcome spontaneity.

No precious thought is lost in the exchange.
What luxury to be able to blurt out thoughts

Simply because they feel important.

Suspended Over a Sea

I feel beautiful and ugly—
I feel beautiful and sad—

A gift   to me   has been given.
Where to place this in my life?

Resentful   then thankful
Opposites abound.
Freedom of choice is inhibited

                    I feel caged.

Will a breathing space open—
A crack of light through the wall?
A flower in my arid desert
A bright star in sorrow's dark depths?

Music is no release
It only sharpens the edge of pain.

Cognitively I travel one direction
Intuitively I wander another.

The power to heal is within—but where?
Finding it is the struggle.

To flee?

To remain?

Suspended over a sea.

Musical Joy

I write music from my heart
sending it into yours.

I write words to announce
what cannot remain silent.

Songs and words of love—
energy longing to be expressed.

Joy searching for release.

Longing, leading us toward union.

Sing *Glory Hallelujah*
for our willingness

To be a resting place for each other

As I hold you   in the

Hollow of my heart.

Life

The simplicity of life

Rests within the bosom of kindness,

Gently cradled by forgiveness

Under the brilliant lamp of love.

VI. DUETS

Trust

I long to feel

The flight of a soaring eagle,

The freedom of a swift salmon,

The unfolding of a tender rose bud.

Lift my boundaries

Fertilize my soil

Relax every cell of my being

      through the touch of your eyes.

I invite you to allow me

      to trust you.

Rejection

Cannonballs of awareness explode

     My glass heart shatters
Slivers pierce each cell

Memories crumble into dust

     Smothering, chocking memories.

The internal earthquake rumbles
Volcano of pain erupts

Spewing blood from my heart

     all over nothing—

For there IS NOTHING left.

Am I a Reality?

Do you think of me often?
Am I a truth   a reality?

Or am I a lie   a deceitful
broken promise?

All is never what it seems

All might be nothing.

Rejection can be acceptance
Hurt can be love.

My spirit begs for contact with yours
Begging is a very bad place to stand.
Intense emotions long to draw you here
into my consciousness   pure desire.

No need to fight

You are protected
By your shielding armor
Of open indifference   masked as grace.

Waiting

Waiting   alone

Looking at one yellow rose and two candles

Waiting to hear the sound of your voice

What will you say?

How will I respond?

Will I say that I have missed you—

That I have held you in my dreams?

Poised with anticipation

Embracing fear and hope.

Conception

Our connection opens
and stretches me

Soul expands and body offers—

Female receptivity beckons

Preparing me to birth
my life's purpose.

Creative brain soil
Waits for fertilization.

Implosion and explosion
Conceiving . . .
The creative act of writing.

A Sea of Flowers

You enter the room silently
And I feel the Earth tremble.

Unspoken   silent   blood racing
I can barely breathe.

Thoughts weave themselves into knots
My speech is foreign to its owner.

Heart pounding, I feel your gaze
weakness spreads
Your breeze blows through me.

One smile from you and

I melt into a sea of flowers.

Sanctity

I invited you to enter the inner sanctity of
my soul—
We grew together in rapid momentum
Remaining, for years, with hearts locked in
love
While nurturing each other in arms of
acceptance.

It seemed impossible for me to begin each
day
Without connecting with your essence.
Like warm milk, your words soothed my
inner hunger,
Allowing me to grow while tethered to you.

You believed in me—totally.

I felt beautiful for the first time in my life
As you showered me with validation
You never treated me like a child
As you nurtured the child within me.

My entire life changed when I joined with
you—
I could breathe freely
And nurture others,
As you have nurtured me.

A Latch

Your voice is soft against my ear,
Soft like the winds that blow across this red
land.

Your voice is warm against my heart,
Like the sun's rays opening me to full
flower.

Your gaze meets mine and my heart stops,
Silenced by the soul reflection in your eyes.

You walk towards me and my breath
catches,
A latch lifts on my heart's gate.

There is a rush to tell you my faults—
Learn them now

      Not after you've touched me.

If this will not be
Please know now

Not after I've placed my pounding heart

      into the curved palms of your hands.

Love Divine

I hear your music and am thrown
Headlong
Into confusion's centrifuge.

Internal pilings rumble
Echoing low vibrations
of my internal quake.

I become less

      and more

as the banality of my human existence
transforms into Love Divine.

Silent Communication

Shelter me

    in the arms of love with no competition.

Shower me

    with acceptance and quiet times.

Let our eyes meet

    in silent communication

And smile with understanding

    at the relief I feel

When joining with you

    at the end of a hectic day.

VII. DIRGE

Five Decades

Five decades of wanting
Five decades of ragged heart scars

Reminding me of the red ric rac trim
mother used to sew on my dresses
Sewing machine needle humming
up and down, up and down.

My blood pulsing
back and forth, back and forth
Heart pumping up, down, up, down

To heal the deep black-and-blue tread marks
– scars on my heart.

Unloving feet blackened my hopes,
stifled my dreams.

If love is the musician's inspiration,
Is loss of love the fountain of pain
from which the poet's words flow?

Is that what finally pulls the trigger,

Driving the bullet deep into my heart?

Surgery

Hammering at the forge of my soul
I wait for mother's surgeon to appear.

Beating the red-hot iron
Pounding my heart
With the maul of my own emotions.

Steaming towards knowing,

The blade of the surgeon's knife
Cuts into my own breast.

But the fire's heat is too low
My soul's iron cooled into rigidity.

As Mom lays in surgery
The ringing of the metal blade
Clangs in my own heart,

Clapper muffled by bloodied pain
In response to my own heartbeat.

On Reaching

The pressure
.... of the years

Cascades
over me like a waterfall.

Swimming upstream
.... against the tide

Struggling to reach
the final goal.

Once there to be swept
.... downstream

In a final rush towards

Death.

VIII. MYSTICAL

Soul Candle

Deep . . . Deep in the cold depths

      of my warm soul

A dim candle flickers.

Flame—hope eternal

      housed in my heart.

Fueled by resolving confusion

Searching for the godliness within.

"Made in the image of God," they say . . .

My reply? "What a responsibility!"

The winds of life's adversities blow

My soul candle flickers.

Divine Reunion

Intense personal pain
Ripping
Tearing open my seared heart—

Raw wound gathering into a unison scream.

Tears bathe the bloodied form
Saline rain flushing swollen emotions into defeat.

The battle is over . . .
Ego descends into despair's abyss

Soul, gazing heavenward,
Longs for the Divine Reunion.

Prayer for Strength

Please help me to be strong enough
Please help me not to be weak,
Let me support rather than lean,
Help me the truth to seek.

Please show me the strength to know myself
Send me courage to cautiously try
To strive for what is "right" in this life,
To question and learn about why.

Why are we drawn and quartered?
By our feelings—so much to endure
With many varying possibilities
To search through before I am sure?

In decades, I hope to look back on my life
And be pleased with what I see—
Give me strength to extend both my hands
With love and trust to those needing me.

Help me to think oh so carefully,
Help me my feelings to know,
Help me to trust, to care, to share—
Please help my wisdom to grow.

Maine Sea Shells

Today I gathered Maine sea shells.

        Some must be female
They have holes.

Others must be male
They're clamped tightly shut.

Small sea creatures lived here
Did they have souls?

Dreamtime

Be still with me, just me and thee
Alone together in the Light.
Friends open your wings, and hear me sing
Of love and beauty, embraced by sight.

Feel the heart beating in your chest
And dream deeply throughout the night.
Let yourself be free and join with me
Find ecstasy in your spiritual flight.

Rest, cradled in the hearts of ancestors.
Allow love to lead you toward the Light,
Along the path o'er life's bumpy roads,
Expand your soul's orb into the night.

We love you, love you—
there is nothing to fear
Don't cling to anger—
don't hold on too tight,
For love is the beginning,
the middle and the end
Of a life spent in preparation
of returning to the Light.

Fly with Me

Come along, come fly with me
Come and feel   Oh! So free,

Listen and hear the sound of the rain
Washing away all care and pain.

Breathe and feel Spirit in the movement of air
As I settle into oneness without a care.

The wind touches my cheek and caresses my face
As I move into unity I shall leave no trace

Of my walk upon planet Earth's own skin,
I can float on the water or dive deeply in.

Tickle my toes with spring's scenes of green
As I dance to life's music to keep my soul clean.

Spiritual knowing feels very light
As I move through the years and the darkness of night.

There's always a glimmer of hope, you know
As we journey through life with so much in tow.

So stand tall, be kind and smile everyday
Allow God's Light beams to show you the way.

Invitation

Spirit be with me in the dead of night.
Teach me to love, to do what is right.

Be patient and lead me up the stairs of knowing,
Help me expand the love seeds I'm sewing.

Let me bloom and flourish. A mentor I want to be,
Trusting in life's process while moving closer to Thee.

My connection with nature's beauty expands deeper and deeper,
As I admire spring's new flowers and listen to the peepers.

Life can be so gentle, or it can whir with great distress,
Help me to remember quiet times, to honor and caress

The very tender moments filled with joy and love,
Moving out of anger, into your wisdom from above.

Love is the greatest teacher, but sorrow teaches us too—
I want to live in alignment knowing all goodness stems from You.

Friends are such precious entities, guides present in physical form,
Accompanying us through this life—until we are reborn.

I offer thanks and gratitude from the depth of my beating heart
For this gift of life You have bestowed and for requiring me to do my part.

Look to the Light

Please let me go,
Please let me love,
Please let me be
With the angels above.

Please stand by my bed,
Please let me be,
Closer and closer and closer
To Thee.

Please come when I need you,
And please hold my hand.
Squeeze it with comfort,
So I understand

That I am your child—
A spark from your flame,
Teach me to follow
As you call out my name.

"Laura, I hear you.
I love you, my dear.
Trust and trust more,
There is nothing to fear.

Stay facing the Light,
Think only of me…
Forward you will move
Into deep clar-i-ty.

Love is the answer,
The path of your way,
Light is the secret
To fill up each day.

Do not struggle too hard,
Truth knows only the Light,
And you will be protected
Through each day and night.

So move into wisdom,
Mentor others—just do
And you will be guided
To know what is true.

Accept the love
Others need to give.
As you cease to struggle
You will learn how to live."

Prayer

When in the throes of despair and pain
We turn to prayer to light our way,
Asking for God's direction and help
As we move forward—day by day.
To believe in a power greater than ourselves,
An amazing Creator with abilities to think,
To comfort, lead and guide us through life,
To pull us back from an encroaching brink
Out of hopelessness, despair and grief,
God opens rays of light to follow,
As a hint of better days to come—
Propelling us forward, into tomorrow.
Life offers a myriad of lessons,
Some most unpleasant, indeed!
Days turn into weeks, months and years
Until finally, from life's trials we are freed.
In spirit form we move into a realm
Of renewal and opportunities for sure!
We worked, loved, prayed and hoped;
We trusted and learned to endure.
We know that bad times can unfold into joy,
There's always something new to see.
More joy, light, beauty and love…
And more growth spir-it-u-al-ly.

Closer and Closer

Smile if you can, even a little
And open your heart to receive
The presence of Spirit—deep in your soul
And all negativity will leave.

Know that you are never alone,
Feel the warmth of ever-present love.
Ask from the very depth of your needs
To receive *peace* from Spirit above.

We become what we choose in life,
Our priorities determine our fate.
Do you support, through presence and love,
Your family, your friends, your mate?

Nothing brings more peace in the soul
Than when we give from the heart.
We are God's voice here on earth,
And we each can do our part

To spread trust, love and forgiveness,
To offer a helping hand,
To care deeply about all we meet
We do everything that we can

To make others' paths a bit smoother,
To inspire, but still share their pain.
When we know that we are *never alone*
Each step forward is another gain.

As we move closer and closer to Spirit,
Closer and closer to Love,
We envision the beauty of Summerland
As we trust messages of Light from above.

.

XI. MELODRAMA

Alone

I live ALONE
and the silence is so deafening
That I can hear the sound
of the snowflakes falling.

I sleep ALONE
and my body waits
To be embraced
in the silence of the night.

I eat ALONE
and am jarred by the sound
of my silverware
scraping my dinner plate.

I come home ALONE
and the sound of the key
Fills the lock to open the bolted door
into the picture-laden room
of silent, screaming memories.

I read alone,
and there is no glancing up
to meet another's gaze...
No exchange of thoughts,
No discussion of ideas.

I write ALONE
and the computer
Holds my emotions—
But no one holds me.

I am ALONE.

Pain

Intense personal pain
Ripping   tearing   at my seared heart.
Raw wounds gather into a unison body scream.

Tears—saline rain bathing my injuries
Flushing swollen emotions into defeat

Ego descends into despair's abyss
Soul . . . gazing heavenward

       Longing . . . for the Divine reunion.

Wishing

How I wish you were here with me today
to walk the damp beach sand,
Leaving our footprints for waves to discover
When the tide returns.

You understand an imprisoned soul,
The withering of my creative spirit
Sucked dry by life's challenges,
Plunged deeper into silence by man.

Here, buried anger surfaces and blows away
Into the soft, gentle ocean breezes.

I am renewed.

Essence

Essence
Webster describes essence as "a state of being."

Being human?
Possessing the internal power to be renewed?
To rise higher?

I paw the soil of my creative soul

Nervous . . . a snorting horse

Searching for my unique essence.

Soul-less

The beauty of a warm, summer-like day
sandwiched between cold March winds
and April's spring blizzards
is such a welcome gift!
Priceless—

Winter doesn't nourish me.
I feel like a person with no soul
A body with no head
A caged woman with no free spirit,

The doors of spring have flung open wide
As wet sands dry in the ocean breeze.

I hear sun-warmed soft, gentle waves.

The wind pauses.
My soul quickens, stirring spiritual energy
. . . moving in my heart as it

Thaws and heals my frozen, creative spirit.

Laura Lee Perkins embraces a lifelong fascination with words and music. Born in Ohio, she was encouraged to love poetry as a child. Laura won her first contest at age nine for a poem titled *My Parakeet.*

Laura received her formal education at Baldwin-Wallace Conservatory, the College of Wooster, the University of Southern Maine and the University of Arizona. She taught in public schools before becoming a Teaching Assistant at the University of Arizona, advancing to positions as adjunct professor for Bowdoin, Bates, Rio Salado, and Prescott Colleges. She also spent six years employed as a magazine editor.

Laura Lee Perkins has authored 150+ published poems, essays, articles and eight books: *A Trilogy, Stepping out of Anger, Dancing on the Podium, Earthmother, Native American Flute Tutor, Native American Songs for Flute, First Light, Lighting Your Spiritual Passion.* In 2019 she published three workbooks: *3 Minutes a Day for 30 Days, WAITING: The Sacred Quivering of the Soul* and *Moving Beyond Fear.* A classically-trained flutist, she produced five CDs: *Sounds of Feelings, Flute Tutor, Bearing Witness, First Light and Heartbeat.*

Laura was awarded five artist-in-residencies: *Turkeyland Cove Foundation* on Martha's Vineyard, MA and four through the U.S. National Parks at *Acadia, Sleeping Bear Dunes, Crater Lake* and *The Great North Cascades.* She earned 3rd place in the *80th Annual Writers' Digest Contest* (Inspirational Category) and 3rd place in the *2017 Creative Writing Institute Short Story Contest* and received 13 grants to support her work.

Laura Lee Perkins thrives on living a split life, writing from the inspiration of Maine's coast (May-Oct) and the peaceful Arizona desert (Nov-Apr). Her public lectures and classes draw 5,000 attendees each year in Maine, Massachusetts, New York and Arizona.

www.ingramcontent.com/pod-product-compliance
Lightning Source LLC
Chambersburg PA
CBHW021153090426
42740CB00008B/1073